Thoughts on
LEADERSHIP

THE FORBES LEADERSHIP LIBRARY

Thoughts on LEADERSHIP

TRIUMPH BOOKS
CHICAGO

FORBES is a registered trademark of Forbes Inc.
The Forbes Leadership Library is a trademark of Forbes Inc.
Their use is pursuant to a license agreement with Forbes Inc.

This edition is published by Triumph Books, Chicago,
by arrangement with Forbes Inc.

Library of Congress Cataloging-in-Publication Data:
Thoughts on leadership.
        p. cm. — (The Forbes leadership library)
    Includes index.
    ISBN 1-57243-058-3
    1. Leadership—Quotations, maxims, etc. I. Forbes magazine.
II. Series.
PN6084.L15T46 1995
808.8'2—dc20   95-8051
                                                            CIP

ISBN 1-57243-058-3

This book is available in quantity at special discounts
for your group or organization. For more information, contact:

TRIUMPH BOOKS
644 S. Clark Street
Chicago, Illinois 60605
(312) 939-3330 FAX (312) 663-3557

Book design by Graffolio.
Cover design © 1995 by Triumph Books.
Illustrations from the Dover Pictorial Archive Series,
edited by Jim Harter (Dover Publications), used with permission.

Printed in the United States of America.

CONTENTS

INTRODUCTION

The moving motive in establishing FORBES Magazine, in 1917, was ardent desire to promulgate humaneness in business, then woefully lacking. . . .

Every issue of FORBES, since its inception, has appeared under the masthead: "With all thy getting, get understanding."

Not only so, but we have devoted, all through the years, a full page to "Thoughts on the Business of Life," reflections by ancient and modern sages calculated to inspire a philosophic mode of life, broad sympathies, charity towards all. . . .

I have faith that the time will eventually come when employees and employers, as well as all mankind, will realize that they serve themselves best when they serve others most.

B. C. Forbes

ABILITY

A community is like a ship;
everyone ought to be prepared
to take the helm.

HENRIK IBSEN

Executive ability is deciding quickly
and getting somebody else to do the work.

JOHN G. POLLARD

Executives who get there and stay
suggest solutions
when they present the problems.

MALCOLM S. FORBES

For success,
attitude is equally as important
as ability.

HARRY F. BANKS

I have always admired the ability
to bite off more than one can chew
and then chew it.

WILLIAM DeMILLE

Life's greatest gift
is natural talent.

P. K. THOMAJAN

One machine can do the work
of fifty ordinary men.
No machine can do the work
of one extraordinary man.

ELBERT HUBBARD

One of the greatest failings
of today's executive
is his inability to do
what he's supposed to do.

MALCOLM KENT

❦

People work for self-expression.
Even when they talk loudest
about "getting the money"
they are really most interested
in doing a job skillfully,
so that others will admire it
and give them that inward glow of satisfaction
which comes of achievement.
From the painter, producing his masterpieces,
to the truck driver, piloting his leviathan
across city streets,
the basic inward thought is:
"I am the best caballero in all Mexico."

HOWARD VINCENT O'BRIEN

Talent for talent's sake
is a bauble and a show.
Talent working with joy
in the cause of universal truth
lifts the possessor to a new power
as a benefactor.

RALPH WALDO EMERSON

Talent is that which is in a man's power;
genius is that in whose power a man is.

JAMES RUSSELL LOWELL

The ability to keep a cool head in an emergency,
maintain poise in the midst of excitement,
and to refuse to be stampeded
are true marks of leadership.

R. SHANNON

The central question
is whether the wonderfully diverse
and gifted assemblage of human beings on this earth
knows how to run a civilization.

ADLAI STEVENSON

The question
"Who ought to be boss?"
is like asking
"Who ought to be the tenor in the quartet?"
Obviously, the man who can sing tenor.

HENRY FORD

The executive of the future
will be rated by his ability
to anticipate his problems
rather than to meet them as they come.

HOWARD COONLEY

ADVERSITY

Great men rejoice in adversity,
just as brave soldiers triumph in war.

SENECA

———

Great men undertake great things
because they are great;
fools, because they think them easy.

LUC DE VAUVENARGUES

———

I have always sought to guide the future—
but it is very lonely sometimes
trying to play God.

OLIVER WENDELL HOLMES, JR.

———

No power is strong enough to be lasting
if it labors under the weight of fear.

CICERO

I love the man that can smile in trouble,
that can gather strength from distress,
and grow brave by reflection.
'Tis the business of little minds to shrink,
but he whose heart is firm,
and whose conscience approves his conduct,
will pursue his principles unto death.

THOMAS PAINE

None think the great unhappy
but the great.

EDWARD YOUNG

Obstacles are those frightful things you see
when you take your eyes off the goal.

HANNAH MOORE

It must be remembered
that there is nothing more difficult to plan,
more doubtful of success,
nor more dangerous to manage,
than the creation of a new system.
For the initiator has the enmity
of all who would profit
by the preservation of the old institutions
and merely lukewarm defenders
in those who would gain by the new ones.

NICCOLÓ MACHIAVELLI

Many of the greatest tyrants
on the records of history
have begun their reigns in the fairest manner.
But this unnatural power
corrupts both the heart and the understanding.

EDMUND BURKE

The contest for ages
has been to rescue liberty
from the grasp of executive power.

DANIEL WEBSTER

⸺◆⸺

The effects of opposition are wonderful.
There are men who rise refreshed
on hearing a threat—men to whom a crisis
which intimidates and paralyzes the majority
comes graceful and beloved as a bride!

RALPH WALDO EMERSON

⸺◆⸺

The men who succeed best in public life
are those who take the risk of
standing by their own convictions.

JAMES A. GARFIELD

The greatest man
is he who chooses right
with the most invincible resolution,
who resists the sorest temptation
from within and without;
who bears the heaviest burdens cheerfully;
who is calmest in storms,
and most fearless under menaces and frowns;
whose reliance on truth, on virtue,
and on God is most unfaltering.

SENECA

The man who is worthy
of being "a leader of men"
will never complain
about the stupidity of his helpers,
the ingratitude of mankind
nor the inappreciation of the public.
These are all a part
of the great game of life.
To meet them and overcome them
and not to go down before them
in disgust, discouragement or defeat—
that is the final proof of power.

WILLIAM J. H. BOETCKER

Victories that are easy are cheap.
Those only are worth having
which come as the result of hard work.

HENRY WARD BEECHER

When ancient opinions
and rules of life
are taken away,
the loss cannot possibly be estimated.
From that moment,
we have no compass to govern us,
nor can we know distinctly
to what port to steer.

EDMUND BURKE

AMBITION

Ambition is the spur
that makes men struggle with destiny.
It is heaven's own incentive
to make purpose great
and achievement greater.

DONALD G. MITCHELL

In every society,
some men are born to rule,
and some to advise.

RALPH WALDO EMERSON

Great hopes
make great men.

THOMAS FULLER

If a man has come to that point
where he is so content that he says,
"I do not want to know any more,
or do any more or be any more,"
he is in a state in which
he ought to be changed into a mummy.

HENRY WARD BEECHER

It is by attempting
to reach the top in a single leap
that so much misery
is caused in the world.

WILLIAM COBBETT

Leadership is the initiation
and direction of endeavor
in the pursuit of consequence.
Anything else is criticism from janitors.

ROYAL ALCOTT

Lives of great men all remind us
we can make our lives sublime!

HENRY WADSWORTH LONGFELLOW

———※———

Man can climb the highest summits,
but he cannot dwell there long.

GEORGE BERNARD SHAW

———※———

The great man
is the man who does a thing
for the first time.

ALEXANDER SMITH

———※———

The power of a man
is his present means
to obtain some future apparent good.

THOMAS HOBBES

The men who build the future
are those who know
that greater things are yet to come,
and that they themselves
will help bring them about.
Their minds are illuminated
by the blazing sun of hope.
They never stop to doubt.
They haven't time.

MELVIN J. EVANS

———◆———

The rung of a ladder
was never meant to rest upon,
but only to hold a man's foot long enough
to enable him to put the other
somewhat higher.

THOMAS H. HUXLEY

Thy destiny is only that of a man,
but thy aspirations may be those of a god.

OVID

———

We don't need men with new ideas
as much as we need men
who will put energy behind the old ideas.

WILLIAM FEATHER

———

What makes greatness
is starting something that lives after you.

RALPH W. SOCKMAN

———

What the future holds for us
depends on what we hold for the future.
Hard-working "todays"
make high-winning "tomorrows."

WILLIAM E. HOLLER

AUTHORITY

Elderly people and those in authority
cannot always be relied upon
to take enlightened and comprehending views
of what they call the indiscretions of youth.

WINSTON CHURCHILL

Lots of folks confuse bad management
with destiny.

ELBERT HUBBARD

Every great advance in natural knowledge
has involved the absolute rejection of authority.

THOMAS HUXLEY

How a minority, reaching majority,
seizing authority, hates a minority.

LEONARD H. ROBBINS

People ask the difference
between a leader and a boss . . .
The leader works in the open
and the boss in covert.
The leader leads and the boss drives.

THEODORE ROOSEVELT

He who is firmly seated in authority
soon learns to think security, and not progress,
the highest lesson of statecraft.

JAMES RUSSELL LOWELL

I will believe in the right of one man
to govern a nation despotically
when I find a man born into the world
with boots and spurs,
and a nation born
with saddles on their backs.

ALGERNON SIDNEY

My liberty is my kingdom,
and here I try to make my rule absolute—
shutting off this single nook from wife,
daughter and society.
Elsewhere I have only a verbal authority, and vague.
Unhappy is the man, in my opinion,
who has no spot at home
where he can be at home to himself—
to court himself and hide away.

MICHEL DE MONTAIGNE

Nothing is more gratifying
to the mind of man
than the power of dominion.

JOSEPH ADDISON

The administration of government,
like a guardianship,
ought to be directed
to the good of those who confer,
not of those who receive the trust.

CICERO

—◦◦◦—

Nothing more impairs authority
than a too frequent or indiscreet use of it.
If thunder itself was to be continual,
it would excite no more terror
than the noise of a mill.

ALFRED KINGSTON

—◦◦◦—

The best test of a man
is authority.

MONTENEGRAN PROVERB

The character of the ruler
is like the wind,
the people like the grass.
In whatever direction the wind blows,
the grass bends.

CONFUCIUS

The general story of mankind will evince
that lawful and settled authority
is very seldom resisted
when it is well employed.

SAMUEL JOHNSON

The man whose authority
is recent is always stern.

AESCHYLUS

The morale of an organization
is not built from the bottom up;
it filters from the top down.

PETER B. KYNE

The power of the state
is measured by the power
that men surrender to it.

FELIX MORLEY

There will never be
a really free and enlightened state
until the state comes to recognize the individual
as a higher and independent power,
from which all its own power and authority
are derived,
and treats him accordingly.

HENRY DAVID THOREAU

Wherever there is a man
who exercises authority,
there is a man who resists authority.

OSCAR WILDE

Work is of two kinds:
first, altering the position of matter
at or near the earth's surface
relative to other such matter;
second, telling other people to do so.
The first kind is unpleasant and ill paid;
the second is pleasant and highly paid.

BERTRAND RUSSELL

CHARACTER

The truly great man
is he who would master no one,
and who would be mastered by none.

KAHLIL GIBRAN

Thou seekest disciples?
Then thou seekest ciphers.

FRIEDRICH W. NIETZSCHE

A character standard is far more important
than even a gold standard.
The success of all economic systems
is still dependent upon both righteous leaders
and righteous people.
In the last analysis, our national future
depends upon our national character—
that is, whether it is spiritually
or materially minded.

ROGER BABSON

Nature imitates itself.
A grain thrown into good ground
brings forth fruit;
a principle thrown into a good mind
brings forth fruit.
Everything is created and conducted
by the same Master:
the root, the branch, the fruits—
the principles, the consequences.

BLAISE PASCAL

A great man leaves clean work behind him
and requires no sweeper up of the chips.

ELIZABETH BARRETT BROWNING

Character is formed, not by laws, commands,
and decrees, but by quiet influence,
unconscious suggestion and personal guidance.

MARION L. BURTON

He is the best leader
who most fully understands the nature of things,
so that his plans are not doomed
to ultimate failure;
who possesses an active, far-ranging imagination
which can see many possibilities;
who has a sense of values,
so that among possibilities
he is able to choose the most excellent;
who has a sense of order,
to give form, design and program
to the values and purposes he selects;
who has practical sense and judgment,
and so uses the most feasible means
to accomplish his ends;
and who has the energy and enthusiasm
to carry his plans persistently toward fruition.

ARTHUR E. MORGAN

If the egoist is weak,
his egotism is worthless.
If the egoist is strong, acute,
full of distinctive character,
his egotism is precious,
and remains a possession of the race.

ALEXANDER SMITH

Forcefulness in the character
of a chief executive
is an invaluable quality.

ROBERT K. PATTERSON

It is energy—
the central element of which is will—
that produces the miracles of enthusiasm
in all ages.
Everywhere it is the mainspring
of what is called force of character
and the sustaining power of all great action.

SAMUEL SMILES

It is not only paying wages,
and giving commands,
that constitute a master of a family;
but prudence, equal behavior,
with a readiness to protect and cherish them,
is what entitles man
to that character
in their very hearts and sentiments.

RICHARD STEELE

It is the character of a brave and resolute man
not to be ruffled by adversity
and not to desert his post.

CICERO

Just as the real basics of human nature
do not change from one generation to another,
so the real basics of human leadership
do not change from one leader to another—
from one field to the next—
but remain always and everywhere the same.

WILLIAM E. HOLLER

Nearly all men can stand adversity,
but if you want to test a man's character,
give him power.

ABRAHAM LINCOLN

"Planners" do not understand
that Civil Service examinations cannot grade men
in loyalty, vision, integrity,
teamwork and tenacity,
which rate even higher than native ability
as qualifications for industrial leadership.

EDGAR M. QUEENY

The great question which, in all ages,
has disturbed mankind
and brought on them
the greatest part of those mischiefs
which have ruined cities,
depopulated countries,
and disordered the peace of the world, has been,
not whether there be power in the world,
not whence it came,
but who should have it.

JOHN LOCKE

The greatest ability in business
is to get along with others
and influence their actions.
A chip on the shoulder
is too heavy a piece of baggage
to carry through life.

JOHN HANCOCK

There is no exercise
better for the heart
than reaching down
and lifting people up.

JOHN ANDREW HOLMES

There is nothing more to be esteemed
than a manly firmness
and decision of character.
I like a person who knows his own mind
and sticks to it;
who sees at once what,
in given circumstances,
is to be done, and does it.

WILLIAM HAZLITT

The most important thing
for a young man
is to establish credit—
a reputation, character.

JOHN D. ROCKEFELLER

CONFIDENCE

A man capable of loving himself
will be like a well-kept flower garden—
productive and inspiring to others.

MARGUERETTE GILMORE

All problems become smaller
if you don't dodge them but confront them.
Touch a thistle timidly, and it pricks you;
grasp it boldly, and its spines crumble.

WILLIAM F. HALSEY

Confidence is that feeling
by which the mind embarks
in great and honorable courses
with a sure hope and trust in itself.

CICERO

Confidence is the foundation
for all business relations.
The degree of confidence a man has in others,
and the degree of confidence others have in him,
determines a man's standing
in the commercial and industrial world.

WILLIAM J. H. BOETCKER

Each man is a hero and an oracle
to somebody.

RALPH WALDO EMERSON

I wonder if there is anyone in the world
who can really direct the affairs of the world,
or of his country,
with any assurance of the result
his actions would have.

MONTAGU C. NORMAN

Indecision is debilitating;
it feeds upon itself;
it is, one might almost say,
habit-forming.
Not only that, but it is contagious;
it transmits itself to others. . . .
Business is dependent upon action.
It cannot go forward by hesitation.
Those in executive positions
must fortify themselves with facts
and accept responsibility
for decisions based upon them.
Often greater risk is involved in postponement
than in making a wrong decision.

HARRY A. HOPF

Keep cool
and command everybody.

LOUIS-ANTOINE-LÉON DE SAINT-JUST

Let not thy will roar
when thy power can be a whisper.

THOMAS FULLER

Modesty is an ornament,
but you go further without it.

GERMAN PROVERB

The greatest mistake you can make in life
is to be continually fearing you will make one.

ELBERT HUBBARD

There is a great man
who makes every man feel small.
But the really great man
is the man who makes every man feel great.

CHINESE PROVERB

They can conquer who believe they can.

VIRGIL

———

We should place confidence in our employee.
Confidence is the foundation of friendship.
If we give it, we will receive it.
Any person in a managerial position,
from supervisor to president,
who feels that his employee
is basically not as good as he is
and who suspects his employee
is always trying to put something over on him,
lacks the necessary qualities for human leadership—
to say nothing of human friendship.

HARRY E. HUMPHREYS, JR.

———

Who will adhere to him
that abandons himself?

PHILIP SIDNEY

COURAGE

A leader of men
must make decisions quickly;
be independent;
act and stand firm; be a fighter;
speak openly, plainly, frankly;
make defeats his lessons;
cooperate; coordinate;
use the best of any alliances or allies;
walk with active faith
courageously toward danger or the unknown;
create a staff;
know, love, and represent
the best interests of his followers;
be loyal, true, frank, and faithful;
reward loyalty;
have a high, intelligent,
and worthy purpose and ideal.
Do justice; love mercy;
fear no man but fear only God.

JOHN W. DODGE

A man is a little thing
while he works by and for himself;
but when he gives voice
to the rules of love and justice,
he is godlike.

RALPH WALDO EMERSON

A man who wants to lead the orchestra
must turn his back on the crowd.

JAMES CROOK

A superior man
is one who is free from fear and anxieties.

CONFUCIUS

Both fortune and love
befriend the bold.

OVID

⸺※⸺

For national leaders,
it is sometimes easier to fight
than to talk.
Impatient cries for total victory
are usually more popular
than the patient tolerance
required of a people
whose leaders are seeking peaceful change
down the intricate paths of diplomacy.

HARLAN CLEVELAND

⸺※⸺

In great straits and when hope is small,
the boldest counsels are the safest.

LIVY

Greatness, in the last analysis,
is largely bravery—
courage in escaping from old ideas and old standards
and respectable ways of doing things.
This is one of the chief elements
in what we vaguely call capacity.
If you do not dare to differ
from your associates and teachers,
you will never be great or your life sublime.
You may be the happier as a result,
or you may be miserable.
Each of us is great
insofar as we perceive and act
on the infinite possibilities
which lie undiscovered and unrecognized
about us.

JAMES HARVEY ROBINSON

It is hard to look up to a leader
who keeps his ear to the ground.

JAMES H. BOREN

Only the bold
get to the top.

PUBLIUS SYRUS

The strength of a country or creed
lies in the true sense of loyalty it can arouse
in the hearts of its people.

LOUIS C. GERSTEIN

The world is not perishing
for the want of clever or talented
or well-meaning men.
It is perishing for the want of men
of courage and resolution who,
in devotion to the cause of right and truth,
can rise above personal feeling
and private ambition.

ROBERT J. MCCRACKEN

Though completely armed with knowledge
and endowed with power,
we are blind and impotent
in a world we have equipped and organized—
a world of which we now fear
the inextricable complexity.

PAUL VALÉRY

This country was not built by men
who relied on somebody else to take care of them.
It was built by men who relied on themselves,
who dared to shape their own lives,
who had enough courage to blaze new trails—
enough confidence in themselves
to take the necessary risks.

J. OLLIE EDMUNDS

This is what I found out about religion:
it gives you courage to make the decisions
you must make in a crisis,
and then the confidence
to leave the result to a higher power.
Only by trust in God
can a man carrying responsibility
find repose.

DWIGHT D. EISENHOWER

DISCIPLINE

Deliberate with caution,
but act with decision;
and yield with graciousness
or oppose with firmness.

CHARLES HOLE

He who gains victory over other men
is strong;
but he who gains a victory over himself
is all powerful.

LAO-TZU

Find a purpose in life so big
it will challenge every capacity
to be at your best.

DAVID O. McKAY

Excellence is an art won
by training and habituation.
We do not act rightly
because we have virtue or excellence,
but we rather have those
because we have acted rightly.
We are what we repeatedly do.
Excellence, then, is not an act, but a habit.

ARISTOTLE

———◆———

Great souls have wills;
feeble ones have only wishes.

CHINESE PROVERB

———◆———

He is great enough
that is his own master.

JOSEPH HALL

He that would govern others,
first should be the master of himself.

PHILIP MASSINGER

I've never known a man worth his salt
who in the long run,
deep down in his heart,
didn't appreciate the grind,
the discipline. . . .
I firmly believe that any man's finest hour—
this greatest fulfillment to all he holds dear—
is that moment when he has worked his heart out
in a good cause
and lies exhausted on the field of battle—
victorious.

VINCE LOMBARDI

If once the people become inattentive
to the public affairs,
you and I and Congress and Assemblies,
Judges and Governors,
shall all become wolves.

THOMAS JEFFERSON

If you wish to succeed
in managing and controlling others—
learn to manage and control yourself.

WILLIAM J. H. BOETCKER

Only the man
who can impose discipline
on himself
is fit to discipline others
or can impose discipline on others.

WILLIAM FEATHER

Power exercised with violence
has seldom been of long duration,
but temper and moderation
generally produce permanence
in all things.

SENECA

The first thing any man has to know
is how to handle himself.
Training counts.
You can't win any game
unless you are ready to win.

CONNIE MACK

The great man
presides over all his states of consciousness
with obstinate rigor.

LEONARDO DA VINCI

There is only one thing
that will really train the human mind
and that is the voluntary use of the mind
by the man himself.
You may aid him,
you may guide him,
you may suggest to him,
and, above all else, you may inspire him.
But the only thing worth having
is that which he gets by his own exertions,
and what he gets
is in direct proportion
to what he puts into it.

ALBERT L. LOWELL

To rule self and subdue our passions
is the more praiseworthy
because so few know how to do it.

FRANCESCO GUICCIARDINI

HUMILITY

All greatness is unconscious,
or it is little and naught.

THOMAS CARLYLE

Consider how many
do not even know your name,
and how many will soon forget it,
and how those who now praise you
will presently blame you.

MARCUS AURELIUS ANTONIUS

Do you wish men to speak well of you?
Then never speak well of yourself.

BLAISE PASCAL

Don't be so humble,
you're not that great.

GOLDA MEIR

Great men never make bad use
of their superiority;
they see it, and feel it,
and are not less modest.
The more they have,
the more they know
their own deficiencies.

JEAN-JACQUES ROUSSEAU

I believe that the first test of a truly great man
is his humility.

JOHN RUSKIN

I do not like heroes;
they make too much noise in the world.
The more radiant their glory,
the more odious they are.

VOLTAIRE

(FRANÇOIS-MARIE AROUET)

I have three precious things
which I hold fast and prize.
The first is gentleness;
the second is frugality;
the third is humility,
which keeps me from putting myself
before others.
Be gentle and you can be bold;
be frugal and you can be liberal;
avoid putting yourself before others
and you can become a leader among men.

LAO-TZU

It is said that it is far more difficult
to hold and maintain leadership (liberty)
than it is to attain it.
Success is a ruthless competitor
for it flatters and nourishes our weaknesses
and lulls us into complacency.
We bask in the sunshine of accomplishment
and lose the spirit of humility
which helps us visualize all the factors
which have contributed to our success.
We are apt to forget
that we are only one of a team,
that in unity there is strength
and that we are strong
only as long as each unit in our organization
functions with precision.

SAMUEL TILDEN

Modesty is what ails me.
That's what kept me under.

ARTEMUS WARD

People who look down upon other people
don't end up being looked up to.

ROBERT HALF

The superior man
is distressed by the limitations of his ability;
he is not distressed by the fact
that men do not recognize the ability
that he has.

CONFUCIUS

There is no limit to the good man can do
if he doesn't care who gets the credit.

JUDSON B. BRANCH

Some persons are always ready
to level those above them
down to themselves,
while they are never willing
to level those below them
up to their own position.
But he that is under the influence of true humility
will avoid both these extremes.
On the one hand,
he will be willing that all should rise
just so far as their diligence
and worth of character will entitle them to;
and on the other hand,
he will be willing that his superiors
should be known and acknowledged in their place,
and have rendered to them
all the honors that are their due.

JONATHAN EDWARDS

The world is moved
not only by the mighty shoves of the heroes,
but also by the aggregate
of the tiny pushes of each honest worker.

FRANK C. ROSS

When we think we lead,
we are most led.

LORD BYRON

(GEORGE GORDON)

IMAGINATION

Genius must have talent
as its complement and implement,
just as in like manner
imagination must have fancy.
In short, the higher intellectual powers
can only act
through a corresponding energy of the lower.

SAMUEL TAYLOR COLERIDGE

Great strides in human progress
are being made by men
who delve deeply into the imagination,
then through the medium of hard work,
bring fancy into reality.

ROBERT K. PATTERSON

I know of nothing sublime
which is not some modification of power.

EDMUND BURKE

It has been said
that absolute power corrupts absolutely,
but may it not be truer to say
that to be absolutely powerful,
a man must first corrupt himself?

TERENCE RATTIGAN

It is not necessary
for all men to be great in action.
The greatest and sublimest power
is often simple patience.

HORACE BUSHNELL

Leaders of men are later remembered less
for the usefulness of what they have achieved
than for the sweep of their endeavors.

CHARLES DE GAULLE

Leadership involves remembering past mistakes,
an analysis of today's achievements,
and a well-grounded imagination
in visualizing the problems of the future.

STANLEY C. ALLYN

Many people know how to work hard;
many others know how to play well;
but the rarest talent in the world
is the ability to introduce elements of playfulness
into work, and to put some constructive labor
into our leisure.

SYDNEY J. HARRIS

The greatest thing about man
is his ability to transcend himself, his ancestry,
and his environment
and to become what he dreams of being.

TULLY C. KNOLES

Real power has fullness and variety.
It is not narrow like lightning,
but broad like light.
The man who truly and worthily excels
in any one line of endeavor might also,
under a change of circumstances,
have excelled in some other line.
Power is a thing of solidarity and wholeness.

ROSWELL D. HITCHCOCK

———◦◦◦———

The beautiful is a phenomenon
which is never apparent of itself,
but is reflected in a thousand different works
of the creator.

JOHANN WOLFGANG VON GOETHE

The lightning spark of thought,
generated or, say rather, heaven-kindled,
in the solitary mind,
awakens its express likeness in another mind,
in a thousand other minds,
and all blaze up together in combined fire.

THOMAS CARLYLE

The secret of all victory
lies in the organization of the nonobvious.
To accomplish great things,
we must not only act, but also dream,
not only plan, but also believe.

ANATOLE FRANCE

JUDGMENT

An executive is one
who makes an immediate decision
and is sometimes right.

ELBERT HUBBARD

Has justice ever grown
in the soil of absolute power?
Has not justice always come
from the heart and spirit
of men who resist power?

WOODROW WILSON

Kings ought to shear,
not skin, their sheep.

ROBERT HERRICK

Most business problems require common sense
rather than legal reference.
They require good judgment
and honesty of purpose
rather than reference to the courts.

EDWARD N. HURLEY

No government is respectable
which is not just.
Without unspotted purity of public faith,
without sacred, public principle,
fidelity and honor,
no mere forms of government,
no machinery of laws,
can give dignity to political society.

DANIEL WEBSTER

Nothing is more becoming a ruler
than to despise no one,
nor to be insolent,
but to preside over all impartially.

EPICTETUS

———

Reason and judgment
are the qualities of a leader.

TACITUS

———

Sound judgment, with discernment,
is the best of seers.

EURIPIDES

———

The country still has faith
in the rule of the people
it's going to elect next.

THEODORE COOK

The law may be set down as good
which is certain in meaning,
just in precept,
convenient in execution,
agreeable to the form of government,
and productive of virtue
in those that live under it.

FRANCIS BACON

The only purpose
for which power can be rightfully exercised
over any member of a civilized community,
against his will,
is to prevent harm to others.
His own good, either physical or moral,
is not a sufficient warrant.

JOHN STUART MILL

The world is governed
much more by opinion
than by laws.
It is not the judgment of courts,
but the moral judgment of individuals
and masses of men
which is the chief wall of defense
around property and life.
With the progress of society,
this power of opinion
is taking the place of wars.

WILLIAM ELLERY CHANNING

Whatever action is performed by a great man,
common men follow in his footsteps,
and whatever standards he sets by exemplary acts,
all the world pursues.

BHAGAVAD GITA

You take all the experience and judgment
of men over fifty out of the world
and there wouldn't be enough left
to run it.

HENRY FORD

Your best hope for success
is that your associates
aren't as good at judging you
as you are at judging them.

FRANK TYGER

Knowledge is the treasure,
but judgment is the treasurer
of a wise man.

WILLIAM PENN

A right judgment
draws us a profit
from all things we see.

WILLIAM SHAKESPEARE

Often a dash of judgment
is better than a flash of genius.

HOWARD W. NEWTON

KNOWLEDGE

A good mind
is lord of a kingdom.

SENECA

One thorn of experience
is worth a whole wilderness of warning.

JAMES RUSSELL LOWELL

A valuable executive
must possess a willingness and ability
to assume responsibility,
a fair knowledge of his particular branch of business,
and a nice understanding
of business principles in general,
also to be able to read and understand human nature.
There is no phase of knowledge
which anyone can safely dismiss
as valueless.

CHARLES CHENEY

It requires a great deal of boldness
and a great deal of caution
to make a great fortune;
and when you have got it,
it requires ten times as much wit to keep it.

MEYER ROTHSCHILD

Great men are they
who see the spiritual is stronger than material force,
that thoughts rule the world.

RALPH WALDO EMERSON

An expert is a man
who knows just that much more about his subject
than his associates.
Most of us are nearer the top than we think.
We fail to realize how easy it is,
how necessary it is to learn that fraction more.

WILLIAM N. HUTCHIN

Any kind of knowledge
gives a certain amount of power.
A knowledge of details
has served in many a crisis.
A knowledge of details
has often caught an error
before it became a catastrophe.

AIMEE BUCHANAN

Education makes a people easy to lead,
but difficult to drive;
easy to govern,
but impossible to enslave.

HENRY BROUGHAM

Every breeze wafts intelligence
from country to country,
every wave rolls it and gives it forth,
and all in turn receive it.
There is a vast commerce of ideas,
there are marts and exchanges
for intellectual discoveries,
and a wonderful fellowship
of those individual intelligences
which make up the minds and opinions of the age.

DANIEL WEBSTER

He who knows
should rule,
and he who does not know
should obey.

ITALIAN PROVERB

If the modern leader doesn't know the facts,
he is in grave trouble,
but rarely do the facts provide unqualified guidance.

JOHN W. GARDNER

The most important part of every business
is to know what ought to be done.

LUCIUS COLUMELL

Study the past
if you would divine the future.

CONFUCIUS

The best of all governments
is that which teaches us
to govern ourselves.

JOHANN WOLFGANG VON GOETHE

In any given society,
the authority of man over man
runs in inverse proportion
to the intellectual development
of that society.

PIERRE J. PROUDHON

The only people who achieve much
are those who want knowledge so badly
that they seek it while the conditions
are still unfavorable.
Favorable conditions never come.

CLIVE S. LEWIS

When a nation gives birth to a man
who is able to produce thought,
another is born who is
able to understand and admire it.

JOSEPH JOUBERT

PERSISTENCE

All rising to a great place
is by a winding stair.

FRANCIS BACON

Big shots are little shots
who kept shooting.

CHRISTOPHER MORLEY

Did you ever hear of a man
who had striven all his life
faithfully and singly toward an object,
and in no measure obtained it?
If a man constantly aspires,
is he not elevated?

HENRY DAVID THOREAU

To be able to endure odium
is the first art to be learned
by those who aspire to power.

SENECA

———◆◆———

Obstinacy is the strength of the weak.
Firmness founded upon principle,
upon truth and right, order and law,
duty and generosity,
is the obstinacy of sages.

JONATHAN LAVATER

———◆◆———

I found that the men and women
who got to the top
were those who did the jobs they had in hand,
with everything they had of energy,
enthusiasm and hard work.

HARRY S. TRUMAN

In every triumph
there's a lot of try.

FRANK TYGER

It is only after an unknown number
of unrecorded labors,
after a host of noble hearts
have succumbed in discouragement,
convinced that their cause is lost;
it is only then that the cause triumphs.

FRANÇOIS GUIZOT

Nothing worthwhile
ever happens quickly and easily.
You achieve only as you are determined to achieve . . .
and as you keep at it
until you have achieved.

ROBERT H. LAUER

Press on.
Nothing in the world
can take the place of persistence.

RAY A. KROC

Real leaders are ordinary people
with extraordinary determinations.

JOHN SEAMAN GARNS

Systems die
—instincts remain.

OLIVER WENDELL HOLMES

Why is one man richer than another?
Because he is more industrious,
more persevering, and more sagacious.

JOHN RUSKIN

PERSUASION

A gentle word, a kind look,
a good-natured smile
can work wonders and accomplish miracles.
There is a secret pride in every human heart
that revolts at tyranny.
You may order and drive an individual,
but you cannot make him respect you.

WILLIAM HAZLITT

Whatsoever moveth
is stronger than that which is moved,
and whatsoever governeth
is stronger than that which is governed.

ST. ARISTIDES

Business today
consists in persuading crowds.

GERALD S. LEE

A leader has two important characteristics;
first, he is going somewhere;
second, he is able to persuade other people
to go with him.

MAXIMILIEN FRANÇOIS ROBESPIERRE

A leader is above all things an animator.
His thought and faith must be communicated
to those he leads.
He and they must form as one
at the moment of executing a plan.
That is the essential condition of success.

FERDINAND FOCH

I've noticed two things
about men who get big salaries.
They are all most invariably men who,
in conversation or in conference,
are adaptable.
They quickly get the other fellow's view.
They are more eager to do this
than to express their own ideas.
Also, they state their own point of view convincingly.

JOHN HALLOCK

It is the first rule of oratory
that a man must appear
such as he would persuade others to be;
and that can be accomplished only
by the force of his life.

JONATHAN SWIFT

Leadership appears to be the art
of getting others to want to do something
you are convinced should be done.

VANCE PACKARD

Leadership is the ability
to get men to do what they don't want to do
and like it.

HARRY S. TRUMAN

Man's rank
is his power to uplift.

GEORGE MACDONALD

Management is the art
of getting three men
to do three men's work.

WILLIAM FEATHER

Not armies, not nations,
have advanced the race;
but here and there, in the course of the ages,
an individual has stood up
and cast his shadow over the world.

EDWIN H. CHAPIN

One of the best ways to persuade others
is with your ears—
by listening to them.

DEAN RUSK

There are two ways of spreading light:
to be the candle
or the mirror that reflects it.

EDITH WHARTON

POWER

A good intention
clothes itself with power.

RALPH WALDO EMERSON

Despotism may govern without faith,
but Liberty cannot.

ALEXIS DE TOCQUEVILLE

He is free
who knows how to keep in his own hands
the power to decide, at each step,
the course of his life,
and who lives in a society
which does not block the exercise
of that power.

SALVADOR DE MADARIAGA

Do you know what amazes me
more than anything else—
the impotence of force to organize anything.
There are only two powers in the world—
the spirit and the sword;
and in the long run the sword
will always be conquered by the spirit.

NAPOLÉON BONAPARTE

———————

I have never been able to conceive
how any rational being
could propose happiness to himself
from the exercise of power over others.

THOMAS JEFFERSON

———————

The depositary of power
is always unpopular.

BENJAMIN DISRAELI

In seasons of tumult and discord,
bad men have the most power;
mental and moral excellence
require peace and quietness.

TACITUS

It is a hard but good law of fate
that as every evil,
so every excessive power
wears itself out.

JOHANN HERDER

It is a strange desire,
to seek power and to lose liberty;
or to seek power over others,
and to lose power over a man's self.

FRANCIS BACON

It is by work that man carves his way
to that measure of power
which will fit him for his destiny.

JOSIAH G. HOLLAND

It is necessary from the very nature of things
that power should be a check to power.

MONTESQUIEU

(CHARLES-LOUIS DE SECONDAT)

Nothing in the world is more haughty
than a man of moderate capacity
when once raised to power.

BARON WESSENBURG

Power is not revealed by striking hard or often,
but by striking true.

HONORÉ DE BALZAC

The culminating point of administration
is to know well how much power,
great or small,
we ought to use
in all circumstances.

MONTESQUIEU

(CHARLES-LOUIS DE SECONDAT)

———◆———

The history of liberty
is the history of the limitations
on the power of the government.

WOODROW WILSON

———◆———

There are very few so foolish
that they had not rather govern themselves
than be governed by others.

THOMAS HOBBES

Those who deny freedom to others
deserve it not for themselves and,
under a just God,
cannot long retain it.

ABRAHAM LINCOLN

Those who seek power for personal ends
eventually run afoul of popular opinion.

CHINESE PROVERB

What is good?
Whatever augments the feeling of power,
the will to power, power itself, in man.

FRIEDRICH W. NIETZSCHE

Though completely armed with knowledge
and endowed with power,
we are blind and impotent
in a world we have equipped and organized—
a world of which we now fear
the inextricable complexity.

PAUL VALÈRY

The only purpose
for which power can be rightfully exercised
over any member of a civilized community,
against his will, is to prevent harm to others.
His own good, either physical or moral,
is not a sufficient warrant.

JOHN STUART MILL

PROGRESS

All progress is initiated
by challenging current conceptions,
and executed by supplanting existing institutions.

GEORGE BERNARD SHAW

———

At every crossing on the road
that leads to the future,
each progressive spirit
is opposed by a thousand
appointed to guard the past.

MAURICE MAETERLINCK

———

In all human activities,
particularly in all matters of business,
times of stress and difficulty
are seasons of opportunity
when the seeds of progress are sown.

THOMAS A. WOODLOCK

Every age has its problem,
by solving which,
humanity is helped forward.

HEINRICH HEINE

Every ship that comes to America
got its chart from Columbus.

RALPH WALDO EMERSON

In thousands of years
there has been no advance in public morals,
in philosophy, in religion or in politics,
but the advance in business
has been the greatest miracle
the world has ever known.

WALLIS E. HOWE

Intelligence and the spirit of adventure
can be combined to create new energies,
and out of these energies may come
exciting and rewarding new prospects.

NORMAN COUSINS

Lincoln was not great
because he was born in a log cabin,
but because he got out of it.

JAMES TRUSLOW ADAMS

Man is not on the earth
solely for his own happiness.
He is there to realize great things
for humanity.

VINCENT VAN GOGH

Progress comes from the intelligent use
of experience.

ELBERT HUBBARD

Progress consists
largely of learning to apply laws and truths
that have always existed.

JOHN ALLAN MAY

Slumber not in the tents of your fathers.
The world is advancing.
Advance with it.

GIUSEPPE MAZZINI

⸺◈⸺

The prudent man may direct a state,
but it is the enthusiast who regenerates it.

ROBERT BULWER-LYTTON

⸺◈⸺

The task for us now,
if we are to survive,
is to build the earth.

TEILHARD DE CHARDIN

True greatness, first of all,
is a thing of the heart.
It is alive with robust
and generous sympathies.
It is neither behind its age
nor too far before it.
It is up with its age,
and ahead of it only just so far
as to be able to lead its march.
It cannot slumber,
for activity is a necessity of its existence.
It is no reservoir, but a fountain.

ROSWELL D. HITCHCOCK

Universal peace will be realized,
not because man will become better,
but because a new order of things,
a new science, new economic necessities
will impose peace.

ANATOLE FRANCE

True statesmanship
is the art of changing a nation
from what it is
into what it ought to be.

WILLIAM R. ALGER

RESPONSIBILITY

A great man is one
who can have power
and not abuse it.

HENRY L. DOHERTY

———◦◦◦———

Cementing the relationships
of the free peoples
is not a job for government
or diplomats alone.
A large responsibility
rests upon all of us.

JOHN J. McCLOY

———◦◦◦———

Economic independence
doesn't set anyone free.
Or it shouldn't,
for the higher up you go,
the more responsibilities become yours.

BERNARD F. GIMBEL

I place economy
among the first and most important virtues,
and public debt
as the greatest dangers to be feared. . . .
To preserve our independence,
we must not let our rulers load us
with perpetual profusion and servitude. . . .
If we run into such debts,
we must be taxed in our meat and drink,
in our necessities and our comforts,
in our labors and in our amusements. . . .
If we can prevent the Government
from wasting the labors of the people,
under the pretense of caring for them,
they will be happy.

THOMAS JEFFERSON

I've got to follow them,
I am their leader.

ALEXANDRE LEDRU-ROLLIN

Life is the acceptance of responsibilities
or their evasion;
it is a business of meeting obligations
or avoiding them.
To every man the choice
is continually being offered,
and by the manner of his choosing
you may fairly measure him.

BEN AMES WILLIAMS

Next to the assumption of power
is the responsibility of relinquishing it.

BENJAMIN DISRAELI

Power flows
to the man who knows how.
Responsibilities gravitate
to the person who can shoulder them.

ELBERT HUBBARD

The price of greatness
is responsibility.

WINSTON S. CHURCHILL

The real danger of democracy
is that the classes which have power under it
will assume all the rights and reject all the duties—
that is, that they will use the political power
to plunder those who have.

WILLIAM GRAHAM SUMNER

There is a price tag on human liberty.
That price is the willingness
to assume the responsibilities of being free men.
Payment of this price
is a personal matter with each of us.
It is not something we can get others to pay for us.
To let others carry the responsibilities
of freedom and the work and worry
that accompany them—
while we share only in the benefits—
may be a very human impulse,
but it is likely to be fatal.

EUGENE HOLMAN

When a man decides to do something,
he must go all the way,
but he must take responsibility
for what he does.
He must know first
why he is doing it
and then must proceed with his actions
with no doubts or remorse.

CARLOS CASTANEDA

When you find a man
who knows his job
and is willing to take responsibility,
keep out of his way and don't bother him
with unnecessary supervision.
What you may think is cooperation
is nothing but interference.

THOMAS DREIER

The best way to teach our young people
the meaning of our democratic freedoms
is to demonstrate, by our own example,
that we have mastered
the "three R's of citizenship"—
Rights, Respect and Responsibilities.

EARL JAMES MCGRATH

❦

There has been in recent years
excessive emphasis on a citizen's rights
and inadequate stress upon his duties
and responsibilities.

PAXTON BLAIR

SERVICE

A dollar put into a book
and a book mastered
might change the whole course
of a boy's life.
It might easily be
the beginning of the development of leadership
that would carry the boy far
in service to his fellow men.

HENRY FORD

An M.B.A.'s first shock
could be the realization
that companies require experience
before they hire a chief executive officer.

ROBERT HALF

He who serves me most,
who serves his country best.

HOMER

If there be any truer measure of a man
than by what he does,
it must be by what he gives.

ROBERT SOUTH

In the high art of serving others,
workers sustain their morale,
management keeps its customers,
and the nation prospers.
One of the indisputable lessons of life
is that we cannot get or keep anything
for ourselves alone
unless we also get it for others.

J. RICHARD SNEED

It should be our purpose in life
to see that each of us makes such a contribution
as will enable us to say that we,
individually and collectively,
are a part of the answer
to the world problem
and not part of the problem itself.

ANDREW CORDIER

Not for himself,
but for the world he lives.

LUCAN

Today's business leader
cannot justify his existence
by profit statements alone.
He must also render service to his local,
national, and world community.

DOROTHY SHAVER

The hinge of fate
has made this nation leader in the struggle
for the oppressed
wherever darkness has fallen
and the light of liberty has gone out. . . .
So live, therefore,
and so perform your part
that free men across the future years
will look back and say,
"Here was a generation
that did not seek security,
but looked for opportunity."

W. NORWOOD BRIGANCE

The leader for the time being,
whoever he may be,
is but an instrument,
to be used until broken
and then to be cast aside;
and if he is worth his salt,
he will care no more when he is broken
than a soldier cares when he is sent
where his life is forfeit
in order that the victory may be won.
In the long fight for righteousness,
the watchword for all of us
is spend and be spent.
It is a little matter
whether any one man fails or succeeds;
but the cause shall not fail,
for it is the cause of mankind.

THEODORE ROOSEVELT

The true measure of a man
is not the number of servants he has,
but the number of people he serves.

ARNOLD GLASGOW

The proper executive
is unquestionably he
who adopts the Golden Rule
as the keynote of his life;
who buries self,
when acting in a representative capacity,
for he is sure so to conduct himself
on all occasions
as to reflect credit upon himself,
and the concern by which he is engaged
as well.

FERDINAND W. LAFRENTZ

The successful person
is one who is able to take his talents
and invest them in the business of living
in a manner that leads to the accomplishment
of a full life of service.

SOL ROTH

Try to forget yourself
in the service of others.
For when we think too much of ourselves
and our own interests,
we easily become despondent.
But when we work for others,
our efforts return to bless us.

SIDNEY POWELL

Virtue

A really great man is known by three signs—
generosity in the design,
humanity in the execution,
moderation in success.

OTTO EDUARD LEOPOLD VON BISMARCK

Do the thing that is right
even when the boss isn't looking
because the boss isn't a criterion.
The real boss is standing alongside you
every moment of your life.

ALFRED P. HAAKE

The more weakness,
the more falsehood;
strength goes straight.

JEAN PAUL RICHTER

Great men are the real men,
in them nature has succeeded.

HENRI FRÉDÉRIC AMIEL

———

It doesn't take great men to do things,
but it is doing things that makes men great.

ARNOLD GLASGOW

———

It is a very easy thing to devise good laws;
the difficulty is to make them effective.
The great mistake
is that of looking upon men as virtuous,
or thinking that they can be made so by laws;
and consequently the greatest art of a politician
is to render vices serviceable
to the cause of virtue.

LORD BOLINGBROKE

(HENRY SAINT JOHN)

It is natural to every man
to wish for distinction;
and the praise of those
who can confer honor by their praise,
in spite of all false philosophy,
is sweet to every human heart;
but as eminence can be
but the lot of a few,
patience of obscurity is a duty
which we owe not more to our own happiness
than to the quiet of the world at large.

SYDNEY SMITH

It is the age that forms the man,
not the man that forms the age.
Great minds do indeed react
on the society which has made them what they are,
but they only pay with interest
what they have received.

THOMAS B. MACAULAY

Noble blood
is an accident of fortune;
noble actions
are the chief mark of greatness.

CARLO GOLDONI

Nothing is politically right
which is morally wrong.

DANIEL O'CONNELL

One should always play fairly
when one has the winning cards.

OSCAR WILDE

Right and truth
are greater than any power,
and all power
is limited by right.

BENJAMIN WHICHCOTE

The shortest and surest way
to live with honor in the world
is to be in reality
what we would appear to be;
all human virtues increase
and strengthen themselves
by the practice and experience of them.

SOCRATES

The superior man
seeks what is right;
the inferior one,
what is profitable.

CONFUCIUS

There are three marks
of a superior man:
being virtuous,
he is free from anxiety;
being wise,
he is free from perplexity;
being brave,
he is free from fear.

CONFUCIUS

They're only truly great
who are truly good.

GEORGE CHAPMAN

A virtue and a muscle are alike.
If neither of them is exercised
they get weak and flabby.

RICHARD L. ROONEY

Good company and good discourse
are the sinews of virtue.

IZAAK WALTON

VISION

A great man
is made up of qualities
that meet or make
great occasions.

JAMES RUSSELL LOWELL

A man without religion or spiritual vision
is like a captain who finds himself
in the midst of an uncharted sea,
without compass, rudder and steering wheel.
He never knows where he is,
which way he is going,
and where he is going to land.

WILLIAM J. H. BOETCKER

If you cry "forward,"
you must without fail
make plain in what direction to go.

ANTON CHEKHOV

Conductors of great symphony orchestras
do not play every musical instrument;
yet through leadership
the ultimate production
is an expressive and unified
combination of tones.

THOMAS D. BAILEY

Great men speak to us
only so far as we have ears and souls
to hear them;
only so far as we have in us the roots,
at least, of that which flowers out in them.

WILL DURANT

It is the spirit of a person
that hangs above him
like a star in the sky.
People identify with him
until there is formed
a parade of men and women,
thus inspired.

GEORGE MATTHEW ADAMS

No one rises so high
as he who knows not
whither he is going.

OLIVER CROMWELL

There are no warlike peoples—
just warlike leaders.

RALPH J. BUNCHE

Power,
from the standpoint of experience,
is merely the relation that exists
between the expression of someone's will
and the execution of that will by others.

LEO TOLSTOI

The future of America
rests not in mediocrity,
but in the constant renewal of leadership
in every phase of our national life.

HERBERT HOOVER

The meaning of history
is never apparent to those who make it;
a leader in any age or generation
is no more than a man who sees
somewhat beyond the end of his nose.

THOMAS SUGRUE

The vision of things to be done
may come a long time
before the way of doing them becomes clear,
but woe to him who distrusts the vision.

JENKIN LLOYD JONES

There is need of a sprightly and vigilant soul
to discern and lay hold
on favorable junctures.

PIERRE CHARRON

We have come from somewhere
and are going somewhere.
The great architect of the universe
never built a stairway
that leads to nowhere.

ROBERT A. MILLIKAN

To face tomorrow
with the thought
of using the methods of yesterday
is to envision life as a standstill.
Each one of us,
no matter what our task,
must search for new and better methods—
for even that which we now do well
must be done better tomorrow.

JAMES F. BELL

Disbelief in futurity
loosens in a great measure
the ties of morality,
and may be for that reason
pernicious to the peace of civil society.

DAVID HUME

It takes vision and courage to create—
it takes faith and courage to prove.

OWEN D. YOUNG

INDEX